GOOD GRIEF

GOOD GRIEF

SALLY ANNE SAINT

Typeset by Fuzzy Flamingo
www.fuzzyflamingo.co.uk

A catalogue for this book is available from the British Library.

This book is dedicated to my mum, Heather, she carried me in her womb for nine months and in her heart always, she inspired me, loved me and taught me so much.

GOOD GRIEF

There is no preparation and no training ground for many of the tough lessons in life. Grief is one of those lessons.

On the 14th December my mother left this earth; at 11.30 in the evening she gave her final breath and with that final breath my world fell apart.

FOREWORD

I first met Sally Saint two years ago when I interviewed her on the *No Labels No Limits* podcast. My initial interest in Sally was sparked by her courageous story and journey that led to the healing and hope work she was doing as a therapist and founder of Conscious Parenting in the UK. Our conversation centered on Sally's approach to "dropping the robe of invisibility" in our lives.

That could have been the end of our interaction. I am glad it was not. I was intrigued and curious how Sally would progress in one of her newer endeavours – sharing her visual art with the world. I realised that the art she created and birthed was an image of her spoken words. It was (and is) powerful – so much so that I asked her if I could share some of it in my community postings. She generously agreed.

Sally and I have continued to stay connected to

each other's respective journeys. When Sally asked if I would write her newest book's foreword, I was honoured to say yes.

Reading this book is like sitting down and having a series of long conversations with Sally over some excellent tea (or, in my case, usually coffee). Sally does the talking, but you hear your own voice echoing the truth within your own soul. If you have suffered the same or similar losses, you may resonate specifically (most of us have if we are honest with ourselves). If, though, you have stood on the sidelines as someone you love and care about to the core of your being is going through loss and grief, you will have an entirely expanded appreciation of the experience.

Over the pages of this book, Sally shares with heroic courage her path and her internal dialogue. Her writing is as evocative as her visual art. Her word choice precise and purposeful. And, despite the title, this is ultimately a book of hope and healing, of emerging from ancestral pain and dehumanisation (from others and self) into the radiance of love and authenticity.

May we all have the grace, courage, kindness, and power that Sally embraced to write this book and to live into her own promise and purpose.

With deepest respect,
Sarah Boxx

Sarah Boxx, bestselling author *The Changemaker Ripple Effect* and the Chief Vision Sherpa for Sarah Boxx Coaching & Consulting where she helps heart-centered action-takers and decision-makers align purpose, passion and values to achieve results in business and life.

CHAPTER ONE

The questions on all lips when I say that my mother passed away: Was she ill? How old was she?

The answers to both are yes, she was ill, she had been re-diagnosed with cancer in the January of 2019 and told that it was terminal then. However, NOTHING prepares you for when they are actually gone.

When you really and truly know that you are never going to physically see them again, when you know you are never going to touch their warm flesh again, when you know you are never going to smell their beautiful scent again, THERE IS NO PREPARATION FOR THAT.

This is my journey, this is my pain, this is my surrendering to the process that we all do our best to avoid thinking about; it is the proverbial skeleton in the closet that we all try and deny, run away from and hope/pray that it NEVER finds us.

The truth is, it does. The truth is, it is one of the threads in life that attaches us all, for we all must face it one day; the reality that those we love and all that is in our life will one day return to dust, like my dear mum's ashes, what remains of the body that housed my mum. Every cell of her body, her laughter, her smile, her pain, her sorrow, her soft flesh, the skin that I know so well for it was so soft, the hair that was on her head, the mole that lay in the middle of her chin. The hands that soothed me a million and one times, the fingers that reached out for mine and the heart that beat. I could lie upon her chest and hear it rhythmically drumming away, telling me that she was close, whispering to me that she loved me with every single beat of it, that she was close and that comfort was mine and mine alone. That is my mum.

In her box, the ashes of a life. It is a beautiful box, warmer than a coffin, closer than a coffin, more peaceful and more her than I could ever have imagined. It gives me comfort and peace in a strange way, strange for I did not imagine it to be so.

The box has pictures of trees, bluebells, sunshine, and a path, a path that leads me through the forest. There are glimpses of the rays of the sun shining through the canopy of dense trees. It is a scene that my mum knows, it is a scene that she has walked and now she encourages me to do the same, to walk the path deep into the forest. Now I walk.

Soudley, in the Forest of Dean, is the location for the picture. It is where my father came from, it is where we, as a family, used to go regularly, for walks and family picnics on a Sunday. The Forest of Dean was in my father's blood, it was in his voice, it was in his veins and it was the gift he gave us all, a love for this area. My mother walked this path because of him.

So here I am, Mum, walking the path that surrounds your ashes, lovely lady. May I do you justice, may you be shining down on me right now and encourage, support and guide my words, for this is another journey we share. For I would not be going on this journey without you laying down your earth body and rising to heaven. Right now this word called heaven gives me very little comfort. It used to, before you left, but right now it is too soon, way too soon. I am sitting here in my kitchen, the hum of my freezer next to me, my legs are cold as it's 2.55 in the morning and I have my dressing gown on, the heating is off and there are tears streaming down my face. I feel no need to wipe them away for there have been so many shed since you left that they have become so well known to me.

The path of tears that travel down my cheeks, warm, familiar, in a way are a comfort, they are my constant companion on this new journey. They are mine; they are my release/relief. The only time I do anything about them is when the nose gets involved! The streaming from there is something that does get my attention.

I suddenly woke from my sleep, and the words 'Good Grief' came into my mind, clear as can be they appeared. So here they are, and in their wake came excitement, certainty and the desire to start the writing process.

I knew it was a book, I knew it was the start and I knew without a shadow of a doubt that I was to start right now. So here I am, dear reader. As I write these words, may we get to know each other and, as I share my story, may it guide you through the terrain of grief. If you have lost someone you will already know that so much of the experiences of grief go unsaid; there are no books that can prepare you and document every single twist and turn that you go through on a daily basis. This book is my attempt to navigate this path with you, to shed light on this journey, to heal my own heart and to support you as yours breaks also and is asking to heal.

This path is not easy; it is not meant to be.

However, it is something that brings so very much with it; there are gifts aplenty. I said to a dear friend recently that in amongst the most pain I have ever felt I have learnt so very much, and as I step back out into this world I want to keep those gifts. This is the good I mean by my title *Good Grief*, this is the secret that I share, these are the gems that are waiting for me on my path, these are the shafts of sunlight that break through the canopy of trees, just like on my mother's box. They are my gifts, they are yours, as you follow this path that leads to who knows where.

This is my beginning, this is the embryo of my book and now that it has started, I feel sleep calling me, I feel my body relaxing, I feel my energy encouraging me, saying, "It has begun, you can now return to slumber, to rest, to sleep, for another day awaits."

Goodnight one and all, the cold kitchen is the start and this pause is so I can return to my bed. It has begun!

23/01/2020

I do not know if there is another chapter; how many words does it take to complete one?

For me, this book is all one chapter, my journey

with grief, my journey with my mother, the love and the pain, the days of stepping one foot in front of the other. The days of life pulling me forward when all I want to do is stop, stop and hold myself. I long for the arms that would have held me a million and one times, my mum's.

Today I had big plans. I had my list. I had decided I was going to tick off all the little jobs that have appeared on my doorstep since my mother passed away. There is the insurance that needs a copy of her death certificate, the solicitors that require some payment and finally the funeral directors, the one that stopped me and my list.

The funeral directors sent the final letter a few days ago. I only skimmed over it when I received it; it contains a printout of all the mourners, and a 'family feedback' form. My head still full of the to do list, I started the form, and like so many, it has the multiple choice options: how we found the service, the support they provided, etc. But near the bottom of the page, it asked for the name of the loved one and the date of their funeral. That sentence broke me.

As I started to write Heather Saint, this wave of emotion hit me, and the tears came. How many more times would I be writing her name? This is the end of the correspondence with the funeral directors, the end of the organising, the end of going back and forth to them with information; it's the end of the 'doing', the end of this chapter. It's done. Once I take the form in, when I hand it over, it's another ending.

My list is on the floor, my plans are no longer on fast forward, I stop and I allow the tears. I allow the hand of grief to touch my heart and make me draw in breaths that hurt, for each breath reminds me that she is gone, that she is another breath further away from me. Every single day takes her from me, every step I take is one away from her and every ending reminds me that she is gone.

CHAPTER TWO

GONE

My beliefs and who I know I am deep inside I thought would have shielded me from this intensity, but they haven't. If anything, they are encouraging me more and more to step into the pain and the grief, to keep acknowledging that my mum has gone. Why? Because it is so easy for my mind to trick me, to pretend that it hasn't happened, so I do not have to feel.

I can fool myself by getting busy, by filling myself with food, by diving into social media, but each time I am encouraged or yanked out of the avoiding and made to feel. Or just encouraged to be, to allow the void, the nothingness, which I must admit can still terrify me. To do nothing, to just give space can completely freak me out!

Right now, in this moment, I am sitting in my

home, in my mum's chair. I call it her chair as it was the one she always sat in when she came to visit me, which was once or twice a week. The chair is deep pink velvet with flowers on, it's the straight-backed kind with armrests and wooden legs, the solid comfy chair.

She would sit here and talk to me, and have lovely naps as it is right next to the radiator, so it's lovely and warm. Right now, the radiator is on, it's winter and it's cold, the comfort, the warmth it gives me must have been the same that she had felt.

This chair and my mum were mentioned in my very first book. I remember writing away opposite her. I was sitting on the sofa, she was in this very chair. My son was on the floor playing with his Lego and my dear mum was fast asleep in this pink velvet chair. She was alive then, ill most definitely, but alive. Now she is gone.

I wish there could be comfort in this chair for me right now, but there's not. It only speaks to me of what was, of who was in there, of what she looked like so peacefully asleep that my heart filled with love just looking at her. It's like the feeling I get when I look at my son asleep. There is innocence when he slumbers, calm and total beauty in the surrender to sleep.

She was here, and now she's gone.

My cup of tea sits on top of the radiator, in the same place I put my mum's when she was here. There is a blanket beside me, a hand-knitted one that my mum got given when she was in the local community hospital being put on morphine. Her pain had got too much to manage so she had two weeks in the hospital to get her on to the right level of medication.

Each patient got given one of these blankets, made up of colourful squares. She had loved the blanket and for me it links to a time when she was more peaceful and relaxed than I had known her for a very long time.

The community hospital was homely, the staff were lovely, she had company and she had her pain brought under control. In those two weeks in hospital, she was surrounded by people she could chat to and who saw her. She had her hair done, attended a lovely group where children from a local school came and made things with the patients. How she enjoyed that, for she loved children full stop.

So the rainbow colours of her blanket remind me of that time, where the constant pain that had gnawed away at her was lessened and she could come alive, she could enjoy colour in her life for a little while.

The tears are flowing again. I need to stop, lift my

glasses up and wipe my face. I didn't think I would be going back with this book. I thought I would only be charting what each day brings, but this memory and this blanket take me back.

When my mother was discharged from the community hospital, it was in just under a week that she went rapidly downhill. It was like watching a car crash and not being able to do anything about it; each day she went further and further down. Her voice was changing as she fell deeper, deeper down a hole that has a final bottom, one that cannot be dug out, one that ends, ends the life of the person falling. My mum.

In the rapid descent, we as a family were completely caught out. My mum could handle pain, she had been riddled with arthritis for years, had had numerous operations and would push her way through anything. Things that would take someone down completely she would fight, get back up and keep going.

Yet the cancer was the final step on her journey to leaving this earth.

I called the doctor out to her and it was decided very quickly that re-admittance was of utmost urgency, and the arrangements were made on her behalf, the doctors organising it all. I spoke to the doctor as she left my mum's house and she said she would do the prescription for 'end of life care' if it was needed quickly on her admittance.

Hearing those words, I didn't register them at the time. It's only now as I type it I realise the enormity of those words. At the time I was worried, in my head I was sorting what needed to be sorted, I was thinking of being strong for my mum and for my family. So those words never landed, I had no response, I had no time for tears, I was doing.

On writing this above paragraph, I realise the importance of allowing, allowing the void, allowing the stop and the silence, for this is one of many enormous moments that went unattended. Unattended as I could not be fully broken by them at the time, so I put up the 'Am not home, am at work' sign, the one where present circumstances are not processed as efficiency and productivity are in charge. No time for emotion!

My mum's care was meant to be at the local community hospital, but there wasn't enough space, so the doctor organised the palliative care to be done at a local care home that provided an overflow service for the hospital.

The facts seem dry, devoid of emotion, they are words on paper, they explain the events but have no feeling, they are directions on a map but not the actual journey.

In fifteen days, my siblings and I watched the descent. Right in front of my eyes, I watched this woman fade, I saw, I witnessed, I cared. I could do nothing to stop the pain or alter the journey. I watched. With the eyes of a woman and the eyes of a child, I watched. For both parts of me and everything in-between I watched my mother go.

27/01/2020

My eyes see and sometimes all too often I say nothing. The eyes and the fingers that were writing the above got halted by the doorbell ringing and I got pulled away from this memory, this moment, by a visitor.

I wish I could say I wanted to see the visitor, but I didn't. I was in the flow with my memory and I wanted to stay there. Yet it was me who opened the door and it was me who sat while my mother's friend talked and talked. My eyes saw, my heart was heavy, but I said nothing.

The visitor was oblivious to my lack of connection with him. He talked away and in doing so he never saw me. So busy was he in his own world that he didn't notice I was not in it with him, and didn't want to be.

The relevance of this was the invisibility, something I shared with my mum, a shared history we have. Most of my mother's life she tried to be invisible for various reasons and so what it ends up with is a person that very few people actually saw.

How many people knocked on my mum's door, sharing their woes, yet how many actually knew hers? How many took the time to see that she was suffering? The visit I mentioned highlights this very point.

CHAPTER THREE

INVISIBLE

The day of my mother's funeral arrived. The day of remembering and of honouring, of feeling, of being with this fact, my mother's body no longer breathing, no longer warm to the touch, no longer soft, pink and moveable.

She lay in a coffin. I love wood but I did not love that box; it was just a box, lifeless and bland. Looking at it, I felt nothing, emptiness was my companion. Just looking at this focal point in the service, the picture of my dear mum in front of this box, did nothing to warm it. There was no warmth.

As her tribute was being read out, my siblings were all named, and I wasn't. I had organised the funeral, spoken to people, got things in motion. It was an error by the person doing it; it is not easy to do a tribute for someone you care about I am sure, but for me it had meaning. INVISIBLE.

How does a child of God get to the state and stage of being invisible, of accepting invisibility as the way to live? Going through days not actually being seen, not truly being seen and known by the people around you.

When the tribute was read there was a murmur from my relations "and Sally". There is no blame, only a lesson wrapped up in one of the most heart-breaking experiences, officially saying goodbye to my mum.

I take that lesson and own that lesson right now. I have walked the path of invisibility, I have needed to do it on many occasions, but not any more. Now is the time to let that path go and speak, be and own my place on this earth as woman, as mother, as teacher, as healer, as giver of life and as sacred vessel.

The willingness to speak, to speak my own words, to be my own mother, to nurture, feed, tend to my own needs is the healing required and I feel could only have successfully been done when my mother left this earth. In knowing I have become the elder of my family, I know it is up to me, no one else, and in that fact lies the balm I need to release the invisibility.

In the act of speaking, I find my own voice, my own likes, dislikes, who I truly am. Maybe the invisibility is in part down to not truly knowing who I am or was. The only way for me to find out is to step forward, make decisions, speak and be willing to make mistakes.

With the leaving of my mum and the entering of my own path, I wonder if it ever would have happened if my mum was still here. Would the shared history have held me in some way? Like the imprints that we all carry unconsciously, would I still have just carried on with this path, it being reinforced by my mum who walked it just about every day?

I wonder if her stoic response to pain was the invisibility way that wrapped around her physical illness as well. Not showing others the truth becoming a way of life, to such an extreme that nothing and no one could truly penetrate.

I read some of my mum's diary recently, and there was an entry about a day she had visited me. She had written that she had wanted to break her heart with me, but she didn't; she said it wouldn't have been fair. In truth, I would have been honoured if she had. We had cried tears together many times, but she always stopped herself from surrendering completely, she always stopped.

It is such a sadness, as I would gladly have held her, like so many times that she had held me. From the baby, the toddler, the teen, the woman and the mother, she had put her arms around all of those stages in my life. Her arms were there, and I would gladly have given mine, time and again I would have comforted her, if she had let me in.

May she be beside me in spirit right now, at this very moment, may she be sitting beside me on my bed, reading these words, knowing how much I love her and may she know that I always will love her. May she be as real beside me as my dog is, who is right next to me, his head next to my mobile phone that is playing Native American music, the drum beat encouraging me with my writing as I match the drumming with the words I am typing on my laptop.

The sun was shining through the window when I started writing. Now is it cloudy outside, the dog's toys at my feet, as I am sitting on my bed. There is comfort here, it feels cosy, warm and full of love. Mum, may you be beside me on my bed, encouraging me with my writing. You always said I should write a book; here I am, Mum, on my second one!

Clouds and sunshine are the same as life, as history, as memories: there are the sunny ones and the cloudy ones and sometimes you have both mixed in together.

When my mother was admitted into the home to receive her 'end of life' care, what happened in amongst the awful witnessing of her deteriorating was something so very magical. My mum found her voice!

For the very first time, I witnessed her speak up. She would straight away say something if she thought something wasn't right. She pulled up anyone she thought was out of line and she did it with such a dry humour it was totally amazing.

It blew me away and drew me closer to her in a way I never thought possible, for it showed me that part of myself that I had been hiding. For everyone loved her. Those who were caring for her had just met her yet they loved her, she was remarkable. Those people were privileged to witness the true unveiling of the most remarkable woman. A woman not afraid to speak, a person unconcerned with what people would think when she spoke; she just spoke, said it like it was and it drew people to her like a magnet.

It was such a blessing and healing for me. It was confirmation and acceptance for a HUGE part of myself that I had hidden. The part I thought alienated me from my family was shown to me in technicolour; she showed me she had it inside her in spades. It was invisible no more, she was invisible no more, she was totally and utterly majestic. She was the divine mother, she was the Goddess, she was the empowered woman.

Wrapped up in the morphine and the tremendousness was THE most divine woman, and I am truly thankful to have witnessed her dropping her invisibility cloak. Do I wish she could have done it in her life BEFORE she was actually getting ready to leave? Of course I do. Every part of me right now wishes with all my heart that she could have done it before and had a completely different life.

Yet the fact she did do it when she was preparing to leave is still a miracle, and a blessing. She gave me one of the greatest gifts, she visibly showed me the difference, the difference in her and those she had contact with.

She showed her entirety and it was amazing; after a lifetime of holding back, of not speaking just in case, she shone. It spoke to me, spoke to me of FINALLY coming home, of being home, of being part of this wonderful woman, of finding out the truth: I AM MY MOTHER'S DAUGHTER. Her embracing of her voice gave me the final part of myself. I could finally accept who I am also.

I am no longer at odds with my past and my path, I see the coming together of who I am, and my place in my family is firm and secure. The denial of myself and the feeling of being at odds with my clan is gone; it was a veil, an illusion, made up of unspoken words and not honouring of self. It's complete and completed; my mother did it.

The good of grieving is something that will be walking with me, over these days, weeks, months and years. Along with the absolute crippling pain, there will be the good, the healings and the blessings. They will knock me down, so I can see them, so I stop, take notice, break my heart in the arms of myself and allow the good, the gift to present itself. As I lay on the floor with pain, a door will open, of that I am sure.

None of us will escape the hand of death, for all those who have wrapped themselves around me with my mum's passing, they know the truth; if they have not experienced this already, they know they will. It is the knowledge that none of us can pass this by that binds us ever closer together. It cuts through any disconnection and illusion, it basically cuts out the crap, it's too real, too deep to be ignored and bypassed. There are so many times I have done my best to avoid the pain, with food, the phone or Facebook, but it is there waiting for me to surrender and allow.

I avoid because every time I break it makes me admit that she has gone, it reminds me that she is no longer physically here. I woke Sunday morning from a dream. In the dream I was talking to her on the phone. It was so real, so very real, but it wasn't.

The desire to not open my eyes was so intense, the tears streamed down and broke through my unopened eyelids. I had to open them, my son and the day beckoned but so too did the reality; I would not be able to phone her. I would not be able to hear her voice, to share whatever I wanted to with her, it was just a dream.

How much I have taken for granted, all those times, all those years when she was there, all those chats about something and nothing, gone. In stepping into each day, it is that which follows me the most. For everything I do and see, all those funny little things, I can't ring her and tell her, I can't hear her voice.

The thought of one day not being able to recall what her voice sounds like any more cripples me. The voice I would have heard in the womb, that would have surrounded me as I grew inside her belly, the voice that would have soothed me, sung to me, told me off, and the voice that reached out to me from the other end of the phone line, gone.

It was the deepest link we had as her health faded over the years; she could still pick up the phone, she could ring, she could be there for me and all her family. She was there on the end of the line, asking how my day had been, what had happened in it and how my son was.

I am so so tired of lies and illusions, so tired of the disconnection that has happened all around us. I have been completely overwhelmed by kindness from so many people, lifts, flowers, hugs, cards, true genuine concern and connection, it makes it so much more apparent, the disconnection that has become so much a part of society and how it functions. So much so that it has become the 'normal' way to live and be.

Yesterday I took myself and my son over to Mum's house. Yes, there were things to sort out, but really I wanted to be close to her, after my dream of talking to her on the phone. As I was tidying her paperwork, I found four unused writing pads, one had never been used, some had only partly been.

The one untouched was one I am truly connected to: the 'Footprints in the Sand' story, which tells the story of a man walking on the beach with the Lord. There are two sets of footprints but sometimes there is only one set. The story tells that when there is one set it is when the Lord is carrying you; the moments when you feel you are totally alone are the ones when he has completely got you.

Here is the story:

"One night I had a dream. I was walking along the beach with the Lord, and across the skies flashes scenes from my life. In most scenes I noticed two sets of footprints in the sand but, to my surprise, I noticed that some times along the path of my life there was only one set of footprints. And I noticed that those the lowest and saddest times in my life. I asked the Lord about it: "Lord, you said that once I decided to follow you, you would walk with me all the way. But I noticed that during the most troublesome times in my life there is only one set of footprints. I don't understand why you left my side when I needed you the most." The Lord said: "My precious child, I never left you during your time of trial. Where you see only one set of footprints, I was carrying you."

I brought home the writing pad, which has a footprint on it and the words of the story. The art of letter writing, of having meaning to words, is something I wish to rekindle. Words can lose their meaning when they and we are disconnected. Too many times I have witnessed and experienced people who are not connected to their words. Somehow, somewhere meaning has been lost.

I don't function that way and I am truly thankful that I don't. When I say something, I mean it. When I write something, I connect to it, full stop.

So, the reclaiming of the writing pad is my honouring of who I am and my commitment to authentic use of the word, and of words. Yes, I will write to people using this pad, I will share this story with others, but truly it's about me honouring and making sacred my words.

Change can only happen from within, so I choose to respect this part of who I am, I respect my own code of conduct with written words. I choose. Which is doubly honoured by me actually writing a book right now! The sun may not be shining outside my window but there is an internal sunshine at my own realisation and acceptance/respect of this aspect of myself.

It is wonderful to respect a part of yourself when all others around you do the same, but it carries even more weight when you choose do it when it is not honoured by a HUGE number of others. There is something about 'The Footprints in the Sand' story that is working with me right now; in the story the man didn't know he was being carried at the time, he was shown after when he was talking to the Lord and they were reviewing the footprints.

How often have I been unaware of those who are supporting me? As I am sitting here, who is supporting me? Who is reviewing my path with me?

The greatest effect on our lives can be that which is not necessarily visible to the eyes!!

CHAPTER FOUR

JUST BEING

I am the ultimate 'doer'. I can organise, sort, see what needs to be done, join 'a' to 'b' to 'c' to 'd,' to 'e'. I think I have made my point! I am known as the 'go to girl'. For anything that needs to be done, just let me know.

Yet in the Footprints story, it shows clearly the effectiveness of something else, something more of being than doing.

My childhood memories are not great about religion and Christianity, but Jesus always felt warm to me, he was never part of my fear of God. He held something else for me, something accessible, something true.

As a child, when I first read the story of the Footprints, it was Jesus jumping out of the page at me and letting me know he was there for me. Now I find him again as I am mourning my mum. When I feel the lowest I have felt in my life at very frequent intervals.

So, he is reaching out me, he is reminding me he is here, but also he reminds me and talks to me of something else: being. Just being.

When I read the Footprints story, I do not get the feeling of effort from it, it's something that just is, something that is beyond doing and more about being. I have this feeling that Jesus is this message and reminder for us all in the art of being.

In being we are free to be ourselves, yet we are also at our most effective. There is no energy wasted in critical thinking of ourselves or others; there is a deep connection to others but not at the detriment to ourselves.

How totally refreshing.

A huge part of my life has been doing, and I know the price for this. There is also a loss of hearing when this is the road chosen. I lost the ability to listen to myself and in so doing lost the ability to deeply listen to others; getting caught in what I thought was right for another meant I was unable to hear and adapt to what was best for them.

Jesus does not seem to do, yet in the being he accomplishes so much. May I start to embrace this part of the journey with my mum also, for she is no longer physically here any more. May her 'being' with me start a whole new journey for our relationship, a depth and a trust. The ultimate guide and travelling companion in my life, for she can no longer 'do' the things she did for me. May I open the doing to her 'being' in my life as I step further from her physical form in my life day by day.

My mum had faith, she regularly went to church and wrote a prayer in her diary every single night, a prayer for herself and her family. Now she is where she prayed to all those years.

To believe in that which cannot be seen, to have faith in something that you don't have to work to achieve. In the just 'being' is the open door, in accepting, in open minds and hearts, in those places of not doing. That's our home.

Many times in life, I have been shown something that asks me to question a fact, or something I believed to be a fact, a truth about myself or life. Someone's passing does just that. Mum's passing has done just that. It pulls questions out into the open and says to me "look at this".

Right now I know I still 'do' too much. I rush, I rush into things, I rush my food, I rush through my day, I rush my thoughts, I get caught in the list of 'things to do' in my head. Which means I drop things and have to redo something, I rush my words, then when I have time to think I change my mind about what I first said.

I feel like a dog that keeps doubling back, like the over-excited spaniel that runs round in circles, knocks things over with its tail and doesn't get very far. What I feel when I am rushing is not excitement, most of the time. Usually it's this pattern that I am so used to. If I feel anxious or unsure, overwhelmed by the things that need to get done, it kicks in; the rush.

It's interesting the word 'rush', as the state I get in when I am doing too much must have a physical response, a hormone/chemical 'rush'.

As I write these final words today, may the 'Footprints' story guide me, for the words written in it do not describe footprints scuffed in the sand by going too fast and tripping up, they are a steady pattern of one print then another. As I add my own story to this tale, I will imagine one print then another, steady and true.

The art of 'being' is one steady foot in front of the other on the beach of life, where each step is visible and leaves its mark.

02/02/2020

The image of the footprints has stayed firm in my mind the days it has been since I last wrote on these pages, the gap between my last entry, which has taken me into a new month. A month which feels like it holds much promise and hope, a new way of seeing things.

The days before were my walking days, walking slowly, so I could really sense my footsteps, where they were taking me and how I was truly feeling. It is really interesting that in this time my body got extremely heavy, so I was physically unable to rush. All was stacked in my favour to slow down and be with each step I took.

I had a dream that was so vivid, a dream that helped me with this time and gave me wisdom to sit with it.

In the dream, both my horses were there. My dear horse called Harry was a gentle horse and for me always represented the feminine. When he was alive and in my life, he showed me the gift of softening, that it was safe to soften, and he loved me.

In my dream, he was standing beside me, but then he went down and lay on top of me. I remember I was concerned he would break my pelvis. Yet even though he was fully on top of me, I had no pain at all. I was lying down with Harry calmly lying on me looking at me.

I remember looking up and Mum was there. I talked to her about Harry and that I was amazed my pelvis was okay. She turned her head to show me something. She showed me Joe. Joe was the other horse I had had in my life many years ago. He always felt very masculine but also wounded masculine. In his life, his mother had rejected him and he had been hand-reared by his owner.

What this meant was an effect on his character. He knew too much, too many human characteristics, and he developed a character that was very determined. He was always the boss horse and could be stubborn and strong willed. He would try to be quite bossy with me too. He developed really crippling arthritis too young, which possibly was influenced by being bottle fed and the trauma of his mother rejecting him, and so he ended up un-rideable and had to adapt to this way of life, until it became too bad and he had to be put to sleep.

It is only now that I realise another similarity between myself and Joe; I was bottle fed as well. Mum said it was one of her biggest regrets. After breastfeeding all her children, she listened to the health visitor and bottle fed me. I was an unsettled baby, so mum was advised to bottle feed and she did. And being a cow's milk intolerant person, this would have been rough for my system but also would have affected our bonding massively. I cried for the first year of life and it was tough on my mum.

In my dream, however, Mum was showing me

how ill Joe was and it was time for him to go to Spirit. Time for him to leave, the wounded male was what I was being shown. My own wounds, my wounded self that bleeds, that knows what it is to fight. The one that will push against any resistance, to the very end.

Harry lying on top of me felt like the feminine aspect of myself was lying on top of me with the full weight, yes, but also there was no fear of damage or pain, it was just necessary so I could not rush to Joe's side and try and fix things, ease his pain, or try to make things better. There was no need for any of that, it was just his time.

My lying down was done with love, overseen by my mum; in partnership with her it felt like she was there to see the process through. She witnessed my wonder at the surrender, when Harry lay me down with no harm done, and she oversaw the process with Joe. She was with Joe when he was leaving.

I have resisted coming to the laptop and writing. I have felt the pull to write but also the desire to avoid, avoid writing these words down and owning them. I now acknowledge the dream, that aspect of myself, the fact I can't avoid it and the reality that it's time to let this aspect of myself die, that which has been a huge part of my life.

The wounded male in me has meant I resonate

with wounded males. Even up until recently, wrapped in the watching of my mother's journey back to Heaven, there were those with wounds around me.

Part of owning my footprint, part of my being, of stopping, is so I have time and space to see what is ready to leave. Another grieving wrapped up in the pain of my mother's passing, like a tornado that sucks up anything that is close to it, another piece of my life is being pulled off the earth and a force as strong as the element of wind is pulling this piece from me.

Now I have actually written this part, I feel more relaxed and peaceful, the avoidance and resistance has eased. In owning what is in my life that no longer serves, in accepting that 'what is' is now 'what was', there is peace.

I wonder if the avoidance is part of the goodbye. When my mother was passing, it was hell; the pain, the suffering, the tears, the frustration, they mark the passing of a life. It is similar with the passing of this 'life form' that was a part of me, that was there for me for a very long time. The fighter, the one who had been hurt so many times, that defence was the automatic shield and barrier to hold back others coming in.

I did think that wounded male had gone from

myself and my life, but maybe the work I had done before only went so far. Maybe I wasn't quite ready to completely say goodbye.

Well, my mum has shown me: Joe is ill, Joe is tired, Joe is ready and in my dream Joe did go. Joe went just like my mum, gone!

The gone leaves something or maybe nothing. I have had this underlying sadness, so in a way the going does get filled. The space where something or someone was does not lie empty.

A sadness that each day speaks to me of acceptance, for each day brings the reality that Mum has really and truly gone. However much I may wish to see her, to hear her, she has gone. There is no fighting of this fact, there is this sadness that walks each step with me.

I can function, I can be there for my son, I can deal with all the paperwork and phone calls that still need to be done with solicitors and other official bodies. Shopping is bought, bills are paid, appointments are made and kept. I can hold conversations, smile, laugh, walk and breathe, but inside I have sadness.

It walks with me, it is there when I eat, it is there when I talk, it is there whatever I am doing, it is my constant companion and that is okay. There is no trying to avoid this one, I don't feel the need to, it is my comrade at this stage. It remembers, it honours that which I have lost, it reminds me of the passing but also that my mum matters.

Every single day it tells me how much my mum matters, it honours her and me. It honours the depth of the connection between us, that which others cannot see or know. This does, the sadness knows it all.

CHAPTER FIVE

CONNECTION

There is such ease to connection when the person you love is alive; everything with my mum was deep. I think it is meant to be, she is/was my mum, there is this whole journey that I have gone on with her.

I grew inside of her, she gave me life, she gave me space to grow inside of her, like I did with my son. I would have heard her heart beat every single day as I floated inside her, it would have been my music, my world, my everything, hearing this sound.

When she was so poorly in the home having her end of life care, I used to cuddle up on the bed beside her and lay my ear against her so I could hear her heartbeat. It felt like this primal connection that meant the world to me and her.

I would lay my arm over her. I had the tiniest of spaces as the bed had a safety rail so she couldn't fall out, but I would squeeze in, and we would just lie there together; she would lay her head on mine and there were no words. She was so tired, but we cuddled up together. I would listen to that heartbeat for hours. Our connection.

It actually feels healthy as I am crying right now, as I write and remember, it feels good to cry. My sadness very rarely brings tears at the moment, it is just this companion. These tears are welcome, for I remember something precious.

The softness of Mum, the smell of her and the thrum of her heartbeat. Being close to her, connecting with heart and not words, makes it so very deep and very special. I will always remember those times.

It was the same when I was growing up. It used to be a Sunday treat with my sister, my mum and I, we would all cuddle up in bed together, Mum in the middle. That went on for years, well into adulthood. Again, for me, I would gravitate to her heartbeat, laying my head where I could hear it.

When I did my share of the chores at home, I used to love ironing my mum's nightie. The heat and the steam would release my mum's natural scent and I loved it so very much.

She very rarely wore perfume, so it was always her natural body scent and it was beautiful to me. I remember she went to stay with a relative for a few days and I ironed her nightie when she was away so I could smell her.

There is a memory that stands out for me, as it was a connection to that something that is so much more. My mum was very poorly and was admitted to hospital. The ambulance came and got her and in amongst all the high emotions of the family who were dealing with it all, there was me. I remember it was my first year in secondary school, the first time my mum had been really poorly and taken into hospital, the first time she had been taken from me. The panic of the family meant they were unable to support me with the terror I was feeling, so I ran outside into a field close to our family home.

Mum had gone in the ambulance, family were doing what needed to be done and I felt so completely alone and scared. When in this field came the most beautiful rainbow, and in the chaos and fear this rainbow told me that all would be okay with Mum, she would be okay.

The calm that came over me, as the rainbow had revealed to me, my mum did eventually come home and was okay. The first moment I remember of that deep connection to something other, something calming, something genuine, something full of love. Since that day, whenever I see a rainbow, they always lift my spirits and give me hope, like it did on that day. The rainbow gave me something that will last my lifetime, one moment, one connection that will continue forever.

As I ponder on this word 'connection', so much comes to mind. This very day I have spoken to my brother and my sister. They are connections in their own right as my family, but also they are connections to Mum. For they too grew in her womb, heard her heartbeat and knew her love.

There are times I find it hard considering ringing them, as really I want to ring my mum and she is not there and at those moments there is absolutely no substitute. The pull is too strong and the pain too intense. However, when it eases, I can then talk to them and we do gain support and comfort from each other.

I also messaged a relative that lives in Southampton. She is older and viewed my mum as hers also, and today I felt the love and connection there as two women who loved my mum dearly. I actually managed to crack jokes in my message and also told her funny things that happened, which I would have told Mum if she had been here. Funny things about my ever-growing son and the hilarious things he had said, what had happened in my week, just little everyday magic moments.

Maybe my sadness is helping with the acceptance

and maybe it allows other people to step in, not as substitutes as there can be none. As individuals who shared love for my mum. It is that very same love and loss that connects us deeply.

I know I have opened up to more people with my mum's passing, I know I have been more raw, more honest and more openly broken, my learnt restrictions vanished. There has also been more clarity and change.

My connection with myself has deepened and with that I have started to make changes. In actually planting myself in my days, I faced many things. I am prioritising me in a natural way, it's not a force that I need to push, it's happening.

As I step into my days with connection in place, I notice. The big lightbulb moment for me was when someone was being disrespectful to me, and in my grief and my doing it had slipped through my radar for quite some time. The beauty for me was that when I woke up my final words to this person was "I deserve better"; how healing it was.

The ripple effect it has was exactly like the mental picture the word ripple conjures up for me, the image of a stone being thrown into deep water and the most amazing ripples expanding from the epicentre, where the stone broke through the surface of the water.

When I actually registered how shoddily this person had treated me, it did feel like a huge stone violating my surface. As I registered not one thing but many, the final straw tipped the scales and, in a second, memory lane went extra fast to show me what I had not connected with before.

So when I spoke those words, just like rippling water it flowed out and out. In doing so, I finally registered many times my boundaries had not been respected and I saw so clearly the moments where I deserved better.

I connected with those words, they connected with me and I am hugely thankful for the person who did tip the scales; he did me a favour as it was so worth it. There is no internal battle to allow those beautiful words to settle, there is no pretence in trying to believe them. I do believe them and it's that belief that is with me every day. Because I connected to them.

So, in my life, I say goodbye to disconnected people, those who are not connected to me. I say: "I deserve better".

This path of connection to myself is opening up. This is a deep one for me, as I know I have allowed awful behaviour from others not because I was not connected to what was happening BUT it was because I was not connected to myself.

In the walk of the rushed life, the ability to register what was actually occurring was severely impaired and I have rushed for a very long time. The link with a hurt and then a response was so dulled for me, it hardly registered at all.

6/02/2020

Now there is very little room in my heart and life for that dulled sensation. Since my last entry, I have been doing a lot of clearing at my mum's. I cannot touch her personal items, but I can do things outside.

I have had help sorting out the sheds full of old furniture, passed down by family from both sides, my mother's and father's. So much of it was absolutely stunning but had been stored for so long it was firewood. Full of woodworm. All this history.

Watching as the man helping me sifted through the piles, being handed relics that were rotten, our family history going on the fire, stirred up emotions deep inside and I itched to get the fire going as more and more wooden furniture was piled up higher and higher. Eventually I could light it and the fire roared into the sky. I watched the flames, felt the searing heat on my skin. I had to step further and further back as it took hold.

There were the words of a song in my head and I sang them as I was mesmerised by these flames. The lyrics of the song are:

"Earth my body
Water my blood
Air My breath
And fire my Spirit"

It was the words "Fire my Spirit" that gained life as the fire expanded and gained so much life force as it became. All that was no longer needed was given ceremony in the fire, the space left is for that which is to be kept. The same for me personally, I realise the hard places I have inside, where my distrust kicks in, or where a learnt behaviour appears, are becoming more and more obvious as I connect to myself and the reality of what is happening. There are so many things to add to my own fire, so my Spirit can rise.

The more I put on my own fire, the bigger the flames and the more space for Spirit to fill, my truth to take its place and my voice to be heard, like the crackling of the fire, true words, simple words, my words.

There is a real energy around the clearing. I remember the same energy appearing when my mum was first diagnosed with cancer two years ago. I channelled it into my son's school, clearing the gardens and weeding, it was my focus and only thing that made any sense, I kept going.

It's the same thing, clearing out, weeding out what is no longer needed, to give space for new growth.

Now I am full of the same energy, to clear, to clear, to clear. I wake in the middle of the night and think about what is to clear next. Thanks to my family being hoarders there is plenty to clear, and because things have been stored for so long there will be more fires, the purification, the smudging with the smoke. All very sacred.

Writing this book and doing the clearing make sense, I am deeply connected to both.

I look at my fingers tapping on the keys in front of them. I am no touch-typist and my laptop is not a new one, so it's a steady process. Yet these fingers connect so deeply with my mum.

Recently my son was reading to me from a fact book, from the oldest tree to the biggest ocean, I was being read the facts. Now I can't remember most of these, but a fact he did read to me is the most beautiful one: our fingerprints are created by what we are against in our mother's womb. How blessed is that!

I never knew this until recently. I knew our fingerprints are unique, I have looked at the swirls on them with wonder, but I did not know that they will forever hold the map of my mum's insides.

Every word I write has her womb printed all over; everything I create and every time I touch someone or something, her print is with me.

The circle and cycle. My son has prints of my womb on his fingertips too. I cannot remember being inside my mother's womb, but my fingertips remind me of the fact. I carry a very special map of her.

CHAPTER SIX

LISTEN

Yesterday I felt disconnected from everything and everyone around me, the dramas, the chitchat, it was like I was there in body but not in Spirit. To all who conversed with me I am sure they thought all was okay, as the ability I have to function was there.

It felt like this separate world was acting out all around me. I was able to dip into it, but I was not actually part of it. It was happening around me, almost like watching a prime time, daytime soap opera. It was TV, so I watched it rather than being part of it, even though I was in the 'story' of the day I was viewing.

When I arrived home after collecting my son from school, I saw that the answer machine on my home phone was flashing, announcing there was a new message.

I pressed the button to play it. It was a utility provider messaging about its service. Usually the machine just plays the current message, but for some reason this time it kept going. It went on to messages left by my mum.

Hearing her voice, I sank to the floor on my knees and wept, to listen to her voice but know I cannot see her, hold her, ring her back. She is gone. Her voice made her real again, her voice connected us so deeply as no matter the content of the message, it was still her and she was alive when she rang and left them.

I cried and cried. Suddenly I was no longer feeling separate from the world, I was back in my body and my heart was letting me know how very much it was hurting. Hurting that the world and everyone else in it is getting on with their lives, moaning, quarrelling about mundane things, making a drama out of everything. I stand around these people and my heart is ripped out.

Anger is what I feel right now, and that is something I find a challenge, in myself, in others, it's something I am continuing to work on. Allowing myself to be angry. Also letting go of this image that something ridiculous will happen if I accept I am angry, like the karmic jester is going to knock on my door, see I am angry and pull the biggest prank on me so I fall flat on my face.

This 'how dare you' karmic jester will then give me back spades of what I have been experiencing.

Maybe that is why I felt disconnected, dulled in some way, the programme that runs inside me and says I will pay. This invisible force that accepts some things and not others, judges some things and not others. Another outdated thought system to listen to, only to acknowledge the truth of its origins and to then choose to say goodbye to.

Perhaps on a fire at my mum's, or maybe it was the last fire that started the ball rolling on this one.

Many years ago, when I started on my own healing journey, I was blessed to connect with two shamanic teachers who used Native American teachings and ceremonies in their work. I felt completely at home, as I had always been drawn to Native Americans, from the books I had read, the pictures I had seen. My whole body registered something, something deep. There was a huge pull to them.

My whole system registered the honesty and love, and I listened. I knew so little, but I loved. From watching westerns with my dad as a kid – he was a total fan of westerns – I loved the horses and the Native Americans in them. I am sure very few of the films were actually true representatives of the truth, but they were my start.

I learnt the facts later, as books came my way from friends, more factual films and my absolute and total love of horses. The healing work came years after the start of my love for this whole view of life, of self, of others. Native Americans listened, they listened to everything. They helped me listen to myself.

There are many times I felt like a fraud: I am a white British female, I have no Native American in my blood. So maybe it was being a farmer's daughter that helped me link with this way, living so close to the land and nature.

There were nine and a half years between my closest sibling and I (I used to say ten years but my sister used to get so annoyed and say it was nine and a half, it made a big difference to her!). I very often felt like an only child because of this gap, so animals became my everything. So much of my childhood was me listening to them, their needs, and in turn they were my closest allies, they listened to me, always.

I do have a memory of a similar connection with my mum. She was walking me to the school bus stop. It was quite a trek and, as she couldn't drive, we went on foot. On this day it was raining, and we were both under the same umbrella; it was the safest, loveliest place to be. Walking with my mum along our drive, the rain making its gentle beat heard on the fabric of the umbrella, me walking arm in arm with my mum. Dry, safe, fields all around us, sky above us, just her and me. Connection and love, plain and simple and unwrapped in a moment with no complications.

It was our own world, for that moment in time, it was just us, no one else existed.

Even now I love the sound of rain. I listen to it on my windows when I am in the house and I always get this inner warmth spread all over me. I feel safe, warm, protected and in this world that is just mine and for those I love.

Surrounded by nature, or a natural force, rain that cocoons me and my family. It's a happy memory.

How a memory can tie itself to something. Rain has become this link with my mum and feeling safe. It has held from my childhood to present day, a link to one moment in time that has become timeless.

I wonder what links there are to come for me, as each day I open my eyes to a new day, days now full of uncertainty, as no two are the same, where the simplest of things can have a profound effect on me.

A lot of the time I feel tired. I am going through a period of not sleeping very well; it seems to be a cycle of restless sleep, then it will ease. Right now it's the restless sleep. I wonder if it's another one of the things that happen in my life which I think are working against me but are actually helping me.

With lack of quality sleep comes another level of raw, more frayed somehow, but also easier to crack. Does this cracking allow me to heal? To stop any attempt at numbing, so I keep on allowing myself to grieve.

I felt recently I had stepped into coping mode, maybe a little too well. It's a functional role but not a heart-centred one; it serves a purpose that actually isn't for my best. It catches my breath when I realise that it's just over six weeks since my mum passed away.

The feeling I have is of others not allowing for my grief. I think it's not entirely others, it's me as well. People can be extremely insensitive, however this experience is one that can only be felt by it actually happening to you, and for every person that is insensitive to me, they will one day have to face exactly the same thing.

I wonder if it annoys me so because I am not allowing myself enough opportunity, and for each insensitive comment it is a reminder to me to be gentler on myself, to allow time. It's also hard that it is people who know me, or maybe only know me at a certain level, which is a truth tonic that is a little tough to swallow.

They are thankfully in the minority. So many of my friends have truly stepped up and are there for me no matter how I am feeling. They do not try and alter my feelings, they respect them and 'hold the space' for me without condition.

It is so damn easy when I see what seems like everyone else getting on with their lives when I am not; the lives I rub up against when I step out of the door and the visual societal message of business as usual no matter what, perfect images, perfect lives, perfect homes sold by social media. How the heck did an app change from an accessory on our phones and laptops to 'real life'?

I am healing, I am breaking, I am feeling exactly what I need to. My mum has gone, this is my truth today and will be for as long as it needs to be.

There was a plan. I decided in February I was going to do x, y, z. The great plan, or actually not that great, just a plan. The thing is with plans is that there is little room to actually listen. A schedule is not the way for me.

What were the chances of my answer machine going into full on play every single message on the machine mode? It has never happened before, yet it happened yesterday. For all my plans, things happen that have more meaning than any plan.

Today I took my mother's and grandmother's

china to a local charity shop. The china that in the weeks of my mum's passing she had asked me to take to a top auction miles away to get the best price. Mum was sure it would be worth a lot, and I agreed I would sort it.

On having it checked out, it was found to be worth very little at all, people didn't want it. I had found the china in sheds and boxes that hadn't been touched for years, braved spiders, mice nests, and decades of dirt. I had carried each piece carefully in the house, laid it on paper, and sent photographs to knowledgeable people.

My dear mum thought she was giving us all a good financial gift, and it was not wanted by anyone.

It was hard for me to box it up today and take it to the charity shop, to admit that what my mum had thought and planned had turned to dust. Her wish to help us after she had gone with the sale of the china had gone.

I know someone will buy the pieces and like the pieces; it will give the charity money to do the great work it does. It's the plan that's gone, my mum's plan. Four people I contacted, but when something is nothing it's nothing, and in the end I had to listen to what was being said. It was worthless.

So many times I have done things in my life and not listened; the consequences of these events have been exactly like the china. I have tried to make something other than what it is, and it is so hard. Hard work, to say the least, when I have kept on giving to the job, person, event, but the giving I was doing was not unconditional. I was giving to get the result I wanted. I kept going to get what I wanted, the outcome I had decided on, not based on facts, when all along it was worthless china.

From atrocious relationships to friendships to work environments, I put the expensive 'china suit' on things that would only ever have a place in a charity shop, so determined to see my predetermined plan through that I ignored the truth and stopped listening.

I wonder if the china is that lesson unfolding for me. I felt it more as I felt bound to the desire to make it happen because it was for Mum, following through on her wish.

Looking back, I have bound myself to men, jobs, my history for sure, when actually they never were that important or wonderful in the first place. My plans were rigid and because I have done it for so long, I can even brace myself against the push back I receive and keep going; in a strange way it actually feels normal to do this hard push back.

When it didn't work, I kept going, when I was treated badly, I kept going, almost blocking out what had happened and sticking to my plan. That man was THE man, that job was THE job.

So maybe, just maybe, uncertainty is exactly where I need to be, so I cannot plan, I CAN ONLY LISTEN. Listen to myself and how I am feeling, listen to the day and listen to its flow.

With my emotions changing frequently, there is no concrete base to go from; I am on sand, which shifts minute by minute, at the mercy of the winds. It goes and flows where the wind takes it. I either fight it or become at one with it, I have choice.

Like the footsteps in the sand I wrote of earlier, that story has just reached deeper inside of me and shown another level. I am walking on sand, so I must listen. Is the wind gentle today? Is it harsh, is it gale force? Is it mixed with rain? I must listen, for my base shifts with the climate when I am walking on sand.

When it is wet sand, after a downpour, I must walk slowly as it can get clogged and stuck to my feet, so I walk slowly. If it's really dry and the wind picks up, pieces of sand can be blown into my eyes and make me cry, my body working with me to remove the painful grain. If it is quicksand I walk on I MUST STOP for I am about to be taken down to my very depths, don't move, don't run, stop and allow.

It feels like my sand is a massive expanse that I

cannot see an end to; this is no seaside beach where the sea, the headland, the walking dogs and people run along. This is a deserted expanse, with no obvious landmarks, nothing to guide me or aim for, no signs of life. This is where I am and that's okay; in acknowledging how I feel, it's actually helped.

In seeing the journey I am really on, there is more understanding and compassion for myself. Others are walking in fields, mountains, swimming in rivers, experiencing many things. Right now, I am in a desert, I choose to stay here and be here as often as I can.

When I visit a friend who is on a mountain, or swimming in a river, I will have more kindness for myself and them. This is my time in the desert, not theirs. I am where I need to be for as long as I need to be.

I walk on sand so I will listen, I will be, I will allow, I will feel, I will heal.

CHAPTER SEVEN

10/02/2020
DEHUMANISING

I was reading a Brene Brown book as I was going to bed last night, its title *Braving the Wilderness*. It is something I have dipped in and out of, as my grief is such that I HAVE to accept how each day will be and acknowledge what I am feeling. Even reading a wonderful book is done differently. Instead of pouring myself into it, it is sitting on my bedside table and I read a couple of paragraphs when I feel like it.

As I started to read, I saw THE tiniest spider abseil down its thread, slowly and deliberately he landed on the thumb of my left hand, whilst I was holding the book open to read. As money spiders go, it had to be the smallest I have ever seen, and it chose me. I couldn't even feel it on my skin, it was that small; no sensation, no tickle, nothing.

What I started to read was about dehumanisation, how and why we do it was explained on the page: when someone is dehumanised it makes it easier to hate them. The examples in the book were race, colour, the atrocities that happened in Rwanda, Hitler, slavery and more, the way groups were labelled as animals and worse, how this labelling meant that it was easier to hate them and treat them so badly, because they were dehumanised.

Yet the door that was opening up inside of me as I was reading was how I have dehumanised myself. The behaviour of others, yes, but also how badly I treat myself, appeared before me, as I read the words from Brene.

I have been in a truly painful place recently, a pain that is so deep, as the desire to hear my mum, to hug her, it's been ripping me apart. The reality that I can't, the reality that I won't be able to, full stop. The fact that no one can ease this pain, no friend or family member can ease this one. This must have opened the door to this truth I have just read about.

In the wanting to have something that I cannot have, it has left me desolate. It also haunts me that I walk in a world where many around me do not understand, for even though my heart is gushing out blood from the break in it, so many people do not see it, they do not see into my eyes.

As the time passes, I feel like the assumption of society at large, as well as those around me, is that it's getting easier, that life goes on and that I am doing so well. It's a non-visible wound. Yet each day that passes takes me further from her, each day is another day where she is not, and it's destroying me right now.

The tears, this gash in my heart, it's ripping me to pieces and so few see it.

I cannot push through it and beyond it, it is here with me right now and it has been for a number of days, for there is nothing to change it. The struggle of each day is mine, the struggle to function when I don't want to. The pressure to be normal when I feel anything but. Just because others forget does not mean I have.

The flowers and sympathy ease out after the first few weeks, the things to do are getting less. It makes way for the reality, that I am walking alone with this pain. My siblings are great, my son is a marvel, my friends are amazing, but I am alone.

Is it this aloneness that has opened up how I feel about myself? For being alone means there is no one else, only me.

In my life, I have known the path of being bullied.

In school it was horrendous, my entire primary school years were torture. Yet I desperately wanted to change my name to the leader of the gang of bullies, Sarah. I thought she had it all, all the friends, the power, everything I didn't have.

My relationships with men have been horrific. In my previous book, I shared in more detail my past; for this book it will be brief. I have been abused, assaulted, and fear has been a constant companion on my path with men.

Yet all this also left an inner scar, of which I have worked on before, but to see in black and white the word dehumanisation I know that I carry it inside of me still. I treat myself as if my words, my body and my heart don't matter.

The ability to push myself beyond my physical need for rest, water, to not listen to its basic needs, to serve other people as if they are my master not my equal, that is where the truth and the hurt lie, in those words. I have treated others as my master.

When I do not see myself as equal to a person, be it male or female, I know I have allowed so many to be my master. I know I have put the opinions and needs of others above my own, to the detriment of my well-being, physically and emotionally.

It's shocking to acknowledge the extent of this pattern.

The truth is hitting me square in the face and jabbing another arrow into a broken heart, as I now see I have been stepping back out into the world with this pattern still working against me.

I have been silent when I should have spoken, I have stepped back and hidden, as another person poured out their nothingness into my space. I am now dehumanising me and it has to stop. For it is flooring me.

The desire to not be around people at all is huge, the pain I feel at some of my connections with others since I have stepped back into the world after my mum's passing seeps into my heart and whispers truth into my ears. So many conversations were way off balance because I stepped back. The other person was my master, what they said, thought, did was more important than my needs.

It has not happened with all people, but it has happened with those who have the ability to completely fill the space and take over: as I have melted into neutral, bland being, they have stepped in to fill the void.

There is a double hurt here, the absolute agony of the reality my mum is not able to hug me and me her, and the hurt at seeing the dynamics I have allowed to be in my life that were not of benefit to me. The links that have been so out of balance and the fact that for all my work on myself, they were and are still here. There is so much more shifting and clearing to be done.

16/02/2020

There is this resistance inside of me.

I resist letting good things in, I feel on edge when there is a gentle day, a pause day, and I try to fill it. I cannot surrender to the calm days; I must fill them with something. Boy oh boy do I have a thing about finishing things, in that I find it hard to finish something. Finishing to me means owning the experience, acknowledging it.

I do all I can to resist lovely things, so I do not receive.

I had a conversation with my sister yesterday. She asked me about my school years and about the girl who bullied me. She had no idea how bad it was, but she said it was something she had wanted to ask me about for a while.

So I told her all the incidents I remembered and she was shocked. In a strange way it has helped me bring peace to this time in my life, telling my story to my sister helped ground what happened. I have written about this time in my first book *The Mask*, where I worked with this experience, but there was another level to this time that is coming out now.

The dehumanisation of myself was compounded by these years of bullying, as the way a bully works and the way the bullied responds is so close to the servant and the master, the under and the over. My world was dictated by another and her gang, my daily life at school was decided by her, I had no free will. As a child, the dehumanisation programme was put in place when I was so very young.

I told my sister the full extent of this time, which I was unable to tell my mum when she was alive for I knew it would hurt her to know. She needed some light in her life and I was it, and so were my siblings. As an adult, my mum would ask me if I had had a happy childhood and I lied and said yes. I knew it meant too much to her and that it would cut her to know the truth, so I didn't tell her.

Mum's life path was also one of being bullied and more. She must have so wanted us all to have different and I am sure my life was better than hers in many ways, and will be because of my willingness to allow change into my life and to open up to others.

It has been deeply healing to speak the truth. It has helped me understand myself more fully and to have compassion for myself, as I now see I still carry so much of the residue of this time.

It's a massive thing to not feel safe at school from such a young age and to not be heard. Unfortunately, I also didn't feel safe at home, so it was a double blow. Both my parents were bullied, so it was my base. There is so much now in the world written and spoken about bullying and its effects, but when I was a child it was not spoken about, acknowledged and no teacher came to my aid. A silent burden.

As I have sat these days with so many uncomfortable feelings inside of me, the epicentre of these was the bullying. How much comes to the surface with the grieving process, more than I could ever imagine.

I sit and wonder at my parents' journey, for in their time physical mishandling of children was more accepted, from teachers dishing out punishments to children who didn't behave, that punishment was inflicting physical pain. To a society that viewed kids as the seen and not heard, hitting and the like was accepted as normal.

How could any sensitive child survive that? Both my parents did, and both were very sensitive; they did their best to bury it but they were.

The only way forward from all of this shared history is self-love, something I came into this world with and like so many the map that was laid before me held directions to the total opposite. Time to rebalance the scales and as a Libran the scales are something I am all too aware of. My desire for balance is something that is always with me and within me.

The bullying at school and other incidents in my life meant I was unable to have the opportunity to listen and respond to my own body, to make decisions about it. I never want my son to walk that path. There are so many things I have learnt and I pray I always have the courage and patience to stop and walk through my past so I do not unintentionally lay out the same path for him.

There is so very much I wish to pass on to my son, but dehumanisation of self is definitely not one of them. May I keep walking the path of self-love, so that fear and the past do not take me back to the old path.

CHAPTER EIGHT

FEAR
18/02/2020

I had a dream last night. I was at home, my family home, my father and mother were there, and the bedroom was like it was donkeys years ago. All of us in one room, the wallpaper was the same, this whitey/cream from being on the walls for years. The flower pattern and the lines that were around the design, was exactly the same, as were the loose pieces.

The loose wallpaper that barely hung on the walls in places, and the potential for spiders to be hiding behind those dreaded places was oh so real in my dream and when I was younger it was true in real life. I was afraid of spiders as a kid and it being a farmhouse it was guaranteed that harvest spiders and the like would be lurking, and harvest spiders are BIG.

I remember when I was younger, we had relatives come and stay a few days. They slept in the sitting room, with the wonderful wood burner still pumping out heat. In the morning, they said they could actually hear the spiders running up the walls! So not so peaceful a night for them!

As a child, we were all in one bedroom, my mum and dad, my sister and me. The room had loose windows, single pane, gaps around the frames, the walls were uneven and wallpaper that had seen better days did its best to stay on the walls.

In my dream, it all came back. I was there again, there was the wooden frame that had been my wardrobe as best it could be, pieces of wood that had been secured to the walls and ceilings, with hooks in the top piece and a strand of curtain wire running the length of the wood so I could hang my clothes on it.

I remember my mum had made two pieces of material into makeshift curtains so my clothes were surrounded by material when they were hung up, so the dust wouldn't get on them.

In my dream, the wooden frame was there but not my clothes. I was standing beside this frame removing the loose wallpaper from the walls, so the spiders had nowhere to run and hide. The task I was determined to do was to remove this wallpaper from the whole room.

My family watched but it was me that was doing it. I was removing the hiding places for fear to creep out.

Now I am awake, it is 11:30 in the morning. I recall that as I woke fear gripped me, and I got up and went downstairs to my sitting room, so as not to wake my son. For I cried, I cried and cried on my knees in this room. Feeling totally alone and scared, afraid I would lose everything.

The fear started to worm its way into my mind and body yesterday, and yes there was a trigger, but it also felt more than the response should have been. Deeper and more crippling. There were lots of tears yesterday too.

It was a blessing that I have a grounded son. He may only be nine and I may be completely capable of fooling many that I am okay, but he knows. He asked me if I was all right and in that moment I cracked and cried. When another human can see beyond your outer exterior and see the truth, it's very humbling. I thought I was acting normally, I thought I was showing no signs of my inner turmoil, but he knew.

I sat on the stairs of my house, as we had just

come through the door after being out in town. He chose the moment we came home to reach out, and it worked. He rubbed my shoulder as I cried, he was unaffected by it, he just held the space for me to cry. How amazing is he!

With the tears and the release, the fear eased, and stayed at bay for the evening, but I woke with it and the memory of the dream.

At this present moment, my whole town is flooded, in a way that I cannot remember. The whole town is on alert and people are deeply affected; some have had their homes flooded. There are many like me who aren't affected, we get trapped by the flood water, but our homes are safe. But the fear, oh my, the fear is horrible. It's almost in the air.

Social media is full of it, the photos, the videos of the flood water, the comments and the worry. There was a comment on the biggest local Facebook page that the water was about to be cut, and panic kicked in. So, I rang Welsh Water, the actual water suppliers, to hear that it wasn't true. I posted on the group what I had been told, and still the fear, people rushing to get bottled water, risking themselves to get water.

Then another comment said the water supply was contaminated, so again I rang Welsh Water. The representative stated this was incorrect, but what she did say was that social media has its uses but people are relying on this kind of thing instead of ringing and getting the facts.

What the whole thread created was fear in people that were already nervous, and it takes me back to my dream. Being surrounded by fear.

My childhood was full of fear, and my dream took me back. In my dream, the feeling of spiders being behind the loose sheets of wallpaper is a pretty horrible thought, but in my dream I had the courage to peel it off. I asked for no one to help me, my family were there but it was me doing the clearing.

Maybe that is what I am doing now, clearing for the family, as my actions in the bedroom affected us all, as it was a communal bedroom. Am I clearing the fear for us all, my father and my mother, my sister and myself, all of us?

My mother and father were afraid, they knew not the power of their own voices, they did not experience the power of the word no, they took things, put up with things, and carried everything in silence.

Here I speak, here I talk to you and to myself, here I go to the places I have not travelled before. To face fear, to face my fear, passed down, lived, carried and trapped by.

It is coming up now, I am feeling it, feeling its

crippling hands around me; it affects my breathing, my being, my heart, my hands and my thoughts. It is this cloak of mist that filters into my very being, so here I face it.

On my island that is my home, my town, surrounded by people who are also afraid, surrounded by flood water and feeding off the fear of all those around them AND on social media, fear breeding fear, it is just like the spiders hiding behind the loose pieces of wallpaper, there hidden but waiting to run out, or hide somewhere else. And because it is where I sleep then I must lay my head down with the thought of the spiders, hidden but ready to run out.

19/02/2020

Is this my path now? To clear this ancestral line?

My parents were brought up under the real threat of World War II, they were both young and involved in the fighting, but war was happening around them. They lived with the constant news of who was lost, who was hurt, who never came home. They were surrounded by food shortages, fear everywhere.

Compounded by the severe parenting that they

both had from one of their parents, they stepped into their adult lives with fear woven into their veins and hearts. They did the best they could but the home they created together had that fear in its nest, its fabric and, as we came along, we were cradled with love but also fear.

So now I face this ancestral fear.

I had a healing last night and what came up was my fear. Almost a mantra deep inside, "I could lose everything". How deep it was woven into my being, and every time my buttons get pushed it has reared its head, whispered into my ear these horrific words. So, I come from this place, I function from here and I dampen myself down in every situation.

On looking at this mantra, I see words that came from somewhere else. When I was growing up, my family were desperately in debt and my mother was the one dealing with the bank and keeping us fed and clothed in this situation. My father spent the money on the farm and the animals, but it was my mother that balanced family life – who to pay and when. Dad hid from this burden.

So, for the majority of her life, she could have lost everything. The mantra was passed from a mother trying to keep her family in the basics, and a husband who denied the responsibility of his actions.

So my inner mantra had its roots in truth at one

time, but now it is no longer necessary to carry it, for it clouds my judgement. I cannot see the way forward as fear grips me with an iron hold. It is time for me to clear this bundle from the past, so I can be free and my son will not end up carrying it too.

I sit looking at him right now. I am on our sofa, he is watching a cartoon and I am typing away. The curtains are closed in the room as it is evening; the house is cosy. A friend's mouse is in the room, as we are looking after him for a few days. The flooding is still a possibility, but I am safe, we are safe, my home is safe.

Here in this space right now there is only love.

The feeling that this flood in Monmouth has created has been total fear. It's the monumental truth that the water will not be controlled, and in some way it has been like the threat my family were under as the war was raging around them when they were younger. Something huge happened around them, something they had no control over, something that would not be stopped, and they could only watch and feel the fear.

Monmouth has been feeling that fear, I have felt it and those moments are awful. My parents lived for years with this kind of fear hanging over them. Would they be bombed, would they be okay, would those they love be okay? It is no different to the fear of this flood. Would people we care about be okay? Would the flood reach us?

The only difference is the amount of time involved, a short-term stress from the flooding, compared to long-term pressure from war.

As I step into my past, and have compassion for my parents' past, it helps me heal my present. The shared patterns that I no longer need to carry around, for it affects every aspect of my life. For when the chips are down, this mantra fills my senses, it floods my being just like this brown water is doing right now to my town. It explodes from me and is all consuming to anything in its path.

Everything in my life is here to help me. The isolation of the flooding, the fear of it, the community terror and my dreams.

CHAPTER NINE

LOVE

All there is, is love.

My son and I have developed our own sign language, and it is for the words "I love you with all my heart". We regularly do it to each other, and this evening I did the hand signs to him and he responded.

This simple exchange took me back to over two months ago, as my mother lay in the nursing home receiving her end of life care. My son could not face the situation, it was all too harsh and alien from what he knew of my mum, so he was unable to cope with visits to her.

However, one day I explained to him that Gran was going to heaven soon and would he like to say anything to her. He did, so I took him to the home, and he walked into the room. I said to my mum that he had something he wanted to tell her. He looked at her and did the sign language. As he made the symbols with his hands, I spoke the words, side by side, mother, son and grandmother, linked by love.

My mum looked at the boy she loved so deeply, he looked down at her and signed his love for her, and I spoke the words, "I love you with all my heart." She tried to sign back as best she could. She spoke a little to him and then I took him away, for he could not stay. The minutes of the exchange took nothing from the depth of connection.

This connection I feel right now and will feel every single time my son and I sign to each other. Beside us as we share this exchange will be my mum. We linked with something deep, pure and ours, our love for one another.

Tears are in my eyes, but love fills my heart.

As the days pass by, the days since my mum left this earth, so much is dropping. All the things I thought were different about us, all the things I thought stood between us, the confusion, the disappointments when I had hoped Mum would have said something different, acted differently. The times I had thought she had let me down, they are evaporating under the light of understanding, compassion and LOVE.

Now she has left this earth, what remains is

love and I can love with depth, truth, honesty and compassion. It is allowing the healing of our shared path to take place, all the turns that were so painful, where I had felt let down, broken and alone. The misunderstandings, the hopes for more, for truer words between us, for deeper conversations, for the walls that stood between us sometimes, all gone.

In the blink of an eye, the bonds that were made from fear have dispersed and now love remains. It is this balm that gently lies down on my wounds and holds me.

The things I had hoped for with my mum, the things I had glimpsed many times, but which sank when fear-based living got its claws into her and me again, are here right now, permanently. It encourages me to go deeper, to step into my mother's past and understand, understand where she came from and why.

To acknowledge that she did the very best she could, that she was human and was the hardest of all on herself; she beat herself up all the time and was locked in her past. Now we are being set free, our relationship is now bathed in light and what is true remains.

As these words are read by others, I hope it brings a glimpse of understanding to relationships, that which I strive for in life, connections with others, but also what I have done my best to insure myself against, for fear of getting hurt.

My desire to protect has been shrouded in the fear, for protection is healthy, but not when it is laced with fear, for fear brings up a veil of smoky nonsense. It's impossible to see clearly.

I have allowed really harsh-energied people into my life, and not even seen the gentle souls. Maybe I was 'protecting' myself from really letting someone in, allowing someone to really see me. My distorted protection was to allow tricksters in, show them an illusion and hide my truth.

Love is the truth, love is all that matters and love has no need for illusions. Protection, of course, but my self-protection allows the deepest part of me to grow, safe, secure and bathed in light. At my core is my truth for I am healing via the invisible umbilical cord from my belly to my mother's in heaven.

We are truly connected, deeper than we were for a lot of our physical life together; we have regained our truth and our life, for I know with absolute certainty that my mother is guiding this healing and this return home, for she knows this is the only way I can truly love.

Truly love myself, truly love others and truly let others into my life for real. She knows she is setting me free of my past bonds, she knows I am healing the ancestral line and she is cheering me on in heaven.

She wanted me to write, she wanted me to love and allow love, she wanted me to be free of the past, our shared past. She wanted better for me than she had, she wanted her grandson to live and be unafraid, she looked at him and saw the free bird he was and is.

Did our paths have to part for this healing to take place? I think it did and I am sure it is the same for so many. For all those who long for a link with a family member that seems impossible to actually have.

I always knew there was more to her and me, that there was a depth, something amazing. In a look exchanged, a hug, the sound of her heartbeat, they were all signposts to the truth. To the absolute and total love.

From the times she would let me play 'hairdresser' on her as a kid, releasing hairspray into a pot of water and combing her hair with it for ages, she let me. The mum who tried her utmost to shield me from all the hard work on the farm so I could read and study.

The mum who washed my toy telephone a million and one times after I had dragged it around the yard on the farm. It would have been filthy, but she didn't stop me taking it out, as she knew I loved it.

The woman who always let me have a pet, for she knew how much I loved them; when one passed and I was ready, she got another. She took the worry of vet's bills, animal food, and I had their love. Which was remarkable when she always worried about getting the money to feed us. She took on crappy jobs and was paid a pittance, so she would have a little extra cash to buy me clothes, etc.

She went without so many times, so I could have. She was up to her neck in work on the farm, but she still did more. She did things for me I am sure I cannot remember, for I expect the family fear put a veil over so very much. I was too afraid to hold on to the lovely, as it did not last, so I must have stacked the lovely away, where no one could get to it and hurt it.

My mum loved, she truly did, but fear was too great for it to have full expression as much as she would have liked, for the love got mixed with fear and created a stew that I am now separating. She was hurt so deeply by so many, she was remarkable to be able to love at all, and she did, she loved many.

Differences, the past, pain, can put up its smoke screens and distort the vision, but behind it all is love. It waits and whispers, it holds the space for each and every one of us.

So many times in my life I did not speak the

words I wanted to to my mother, I never told her the extent of my bullying as a child, as I did not want to upset a woman who was already hurting so much, so I hid it. I did not say that her ringing two or three times a day was too much, as it would hurt a woman that was already hurting.

I did not reach out and hold her until she allowed herself to truly break, to cry, for I knew if I did she would allow out a lifetime of pain and it would hurt, hurt so much it could break her.

It was only with the morphine coming into her pain-riddled body that she started the process of letting go, of letting go of the bodily pain and the worldly, a lifetime of pain was slowly being laid to rest.

I wish I could hold her, see her right now, but I must embrace what is here, not what was. Her love remains, in the eyes of my son and in my heart. In my sister's voice and my brother's presence, in the family home that still houses her personal items. In my cousins, in the friends that knew us both, they all carry her torch and they all carry her love.

Love is the truth, everything us is a bundle of the past, it is not real, it will never speak the truth and will only hold us back.

Step into the truth and step into your life, as I am stepping into mine. I know there are more illusions to shatter, there is more past to see and release. I know they are all here on my path of grieving BUT I also know this is the path of love. This is the gift, the gift of grieving, the gift of truly living. It is love.

At forty-seven, I open up to the truth and accept the path I am on, to allow love into my life and my heart to beam it permanently. I know to do this I must be brave, I must be broken, I must weep, I must surrender. I know this will be my path for many moons to come, but now the path is illuminated.

I did not know this was the way and what was happening when I started writing this book. I did not know this was the gift when the title of the book appeared in my consciousness. Yet here it is. It is in saying yes to the journey that the path opens up, it is in trusting and having faith that the steps of the journey unfold. It is in opening up to our ancestors with understanding that we truly gain understanding and peace with our pasts.

This book is dedicated to love, to the love for my mother and the love she has for me. It is dedicated to the new path we are on, different to the past as we are both free to live in our truths. Love is at our core, love is our relationship, love is our truth. We walk together still; we are connected even deeper than when she was 'alive', and we will never be parted or have anything come between us.

There are no cross words, there are no misunderstandings, there is no loss. There is only love. We have not lost each other, we have regained and reclaimed our truth; we are bonded in the dance of eternal love and light.

Peace to you all, connection to you all, love to you all. Walk the path and allow love in. A physical death is not the end, it is just the beginning.

Printed in Great Britain
by Amazon

45195143R00056